Through the Fire

A Memoir of Trauma and Loss, Basketball and Triumph

Scott Williams
and Ben Guest

ISBN: 979-8386920999

Copyright © 2023 Scott Williams

All rights reserved. No part of this book may be reproduced or transmitted in any form or by any means, electronic or mechanical, including photocopying and recording, or by any information storage and retrieval system, without permission in writing from the publisher.

Published By: Books For Athletes www.BooksForAthletes.com

With love to: Lisa, Benjamin & Ava.

And to my Mom.

I know you're afraid of what you feel You still need time to heal

Through whatever, come what may I'd take it all the way

Right down to the wire

Even through the fire

- "Through the Fire"
by Chaka Khan

CONTENTS

Part I: Hacienda Heights 7

Prologue 8
Chapter 1: Epiphany 9
Chapter 2: Growing Up 15

Part II: Chapel Hill 25

Chapter 3: Freshman Year 27
Chapter 4: Tragedy 37
Chapter 5: Carolina Family 41
Chapter 6: Undrafted 51

Part III: Chicago 55

Chapter 7: Training Camp 57
Chapter 8: Michael Jordan 83
Chapter 9: Running with the Bulls 95

Part IV: The League 111

Chapter 10: Around the League 113
Chapter 11: Always Be Pro 119
Chapter 12: Jordan versus LeBron 129

Part V: Through the Fire 137

Chapter 13: Little Victories 139

Chapter 14: $200 143
Chapter 15: Ben and Ava.. 145
Chapter 16: Mom.. 147

Part I:
Hacienda Heights

PROLOGUE

One night, as a child, I awoke to find my father standing in my room, in the dark, staring at me.

For a long time after that, I would balance pots and pans in front of my bedroom door so that if he came back they would fall over and wake me.

I never told anyone this but until I was eighteen years old I wet the bed.

Through senior year of high school, I slept on a mattress covered with plastic and it was only when I left home for college that my bed-wetting stopped.

It took me years to put two and two together.

CHAPTER 1

Epiphany

1992.

The buzzer sounds.

I throw my arms to the ceiling and look around for a teammate to hug.

Bill Cartwright, who us younger guys call "Teach," is the closest one to me and I grab him in an embrace, both of us wearing our white Chicago Bulls uniforms, sweaty from the comeback we had just completed.

Winning an NBA championship is a high you can't recreate. Not from sex, not from drugs, not from money. It's the culmination of so much hard work in the face of so many sacrifices and so many setbacks.

People say the birth of your child is the greatest feeling. Being a father has brought me more joy than anything in life but winning a championship is the single greatest rush a person can experience.

We make our way through the celebrating fans to the tunnel and down the staircase to our locker room below. It smells like state fair down there, popcorn and beer and Polish hot dogs, all stored beneath the stadium for the fans in their red courtside seats.

I'm an undrafted free agent in my second year in the National Basketball Association. I'm on a minimum, non-guaranteed, contract and I had just played the entire fourth quarter of Game 6 of the 1992 NBA Finals, one of the greatest comebacks in Finals history, beating the Portland Trail Blazers 97 to 93.

In the most important quarter of our season, the championship-winning quarter, I was the only reserve, the only one of the "bench bunch," to play all twelve minutes. In the biggest moment of the season, I got the call.

At the start of the fourth quarter, we were down fifteen points. Coach Phil Jackson, "PJ," had thrown in the towel, subbing all the starters except for Scottie Pippen. While Michael Jordan, the greatest player of all-time, cheered us on from the bench my teammates and I got us back in the game.

Bobby Hansen started the rally by hitting a three to start the quarter. Pip got free inside. Stacey King scored off glass. B.J. Armstrong hit a jumper from the baseline. I blocked Clyde Drexler at the rim and, like that, the blazer's lead was down to four. PJ regained the faith and, with eight minutes left, put Jordan back in.

Looking at MJ, the "Black Cat," and then looking over at the Blazers, their shoulders slumped as Jordan stepped onto the court, I had one thought:

Have a nice flight home.

Jordan scored twelve of the next nineteen points and we won by four. It was the greatest fourth quarter NBA Finals comeback in league history and I was the only Bull to play the entire quarter.

Back-to-back champions.

Childhood emotions of playing on the playground and winning a championship flood through me.

"Go to the Blackhawks locker room," someone shouts.

Chicago Stadium was built in 1929 for the Chicago Blackhawks, back when the popularity of the National Hockey League dwarfed that of the National Basketball Association. The Chicago Bulls came along 40 years later and we've been playing the red-headed step-child ever since. Now our shoebox of a locker room is too small for the NBC television cameras.

We make our way down the black and white checkerboard-tiled hallway to the Blackhawk's locker room. David Stern, the commissioner of the NBA, and Bob Costas, from NBC, wait to present us with the L.O.B., the Larry O'Brien Championship Trophy.

Before that can happen, PJ and Craig Hodges, our veteran three-point marksman, call us together for the Lord's Prayer.

We huddle up for the final time of the season. I put my arms around my teammates. My *brothers*.

At twenty-four years old, they are some of the only family I have left.

"Thy kingdom come; thy will be done…"

We finish the prayer and the champagne showers begin.

As Costas interviews Jordan and Pippen the word comes down: *The fans aren't leaving.*

We go back up the stairs and emerge into Chicago Stadium, the cheers raining down on us like confetti.

The entire team jumps up on the scorer's table, standing on the red covering, dancing and celebrating with the crowd, Gary Glitter's "Rock and Roll Part 2" blaring over the sound system.

My white championship t-shirt, "NBA WORLD CHAMPS BACK-TO-BACK," and black Adidas are soaked with champagne.

"Hey!" sings Glitter as the entire stadium shouts "Hey!" in unison.

Last year we closed out the Finals in Los Angeles so this is our first championship at home.

"Tank," says Pippen, standing next to me, calling my nickname as he hands me the L.O.B.

I hold the trophy above my head.

Two years in the league, two championships, chips as big as the ones on my shoulders.

I feel a sense of pride and a sense relief at the same time. All season long I had played "closer" minutes in the most important games.

"Heyyyyyyy!" everyone shouts.

As I stand there, holding the trophy, Scottie Pippen and Michael Jordan by my side, 16,600 Chicagoans cheering us on, I have an epiphany. *It doesn't matter how I got here, I belong.*

"I can play in this league," I think.

"I can play in this league as long as I want."

"Heyyyyyyyyyyyy!"

CHAPTER 2

Growing Up

Our address was 16636 Echo Hill Way, Hacienda Heights, a middle-class suburb of Los Angeles.

In front of our brown, two-story house sat Mom's money green Volvo and Dad's light blue Cadillac with all-white leather interior. Sago palms stood at attention on either side of our walkway and a basketball hoop hung over the middle garage.

In the backyard there was a swimming pool, jacuzzi, and fire pit. My friends and I would sit in the jacuzzi, jump up out the hot water, into the cold water of the pool, and then run around the deck and jump back in the jacuzzi.

Hot and cold.

My mom's name was Claire, but everyone called her Rita. She grew up in Asbury Park, New Jersey. Her mother, my grandmother, was a high school teacher and vice-principal and the family moved to California when my mom was still a teenager.

My Mom was a cashier at Alpha Beta, a local grocery store, and the PTA board secretary. Five-ten with dimples, she made friends easily, loved music, and loved to sing along to Earth, Wind, and Fire.

One of her favorite songs was "September."

> Our hearts were ringing
> In the key that our souls were singing
> As we danced in the night
> Remember how the stars stole the night away

My parents married young, my mom eighteen and my dad twenty-one.

Mom was pregnant with my older brother, Chip, and, in those days, if you got someone pregnant you generally got married.

My father Al, short for Albert, was a monster. He resented us, resented he couldn't live life as a single man, free from obligation.

My father grew up in L.A., grew up in an abusive family. He worked at Sears as a big box salesman, washers and dryers mostly. He wore a "piece" to cover his bald spot; he wore a mask to cover his rage.

He had been abused so he abused all of us. He would start by yelling, an inferno that could be set off by any spark. The yelling led to cursing and the cursing led to beatings.

Not spankings but *beatings*.

Belts mostly, but anything he could get to quickly was in play. He once hit my brother across the head with a jug of wine in a hotel room in Hawaii. Chip collapsed, blood gushing from his head.

In that moment I thought my brother was dead.

I've never gotten that image out of my mind. The blood from my brother's head. The hotel security. The lies.

It was a living nightmare.

—

My dad was the assistant coach for my little league team. When my teammates came over to the house he'd put on his blue Dodger's hat.

"Get my hat," he'd say, almost frantic. "Get my hat, get my hat," not wanting anyone to see him for who he really was.

THROUGH THE FIRE

To my friends and my teammates, he was the cool dad who was always around, the dad who hit grounders and manned the grill. Sometimes they would say, "I wish I had your dad."

"No," I said, "you don't."

I never told anyone what we were going through. In an abusive household, shame and fear are silent partners.

My mother was working late one warm summer night when I was twelve and Chip fifteen. I can't remember what set my father off, but he was yelling and cursing and we knew what came next.

I had the key to the Jackson's house down the street. They were on vacation and it was my job to feed their fish and water their plants. My brother and I slipped out of our house, dangling out a window on the second floor, above the garage. Chip lowered me to the ground by my hands. He hung from the side of the roof and dropped next to me.

We sat in the dark in our neighbors' living room for hours. I kept watch, peeking out through the drapes, afraid of my father, keeping an eye on our home and for my mom's green Volvo.

We were never safe.

—

As a child my two favorite TV shows were *Love Boat* and *Fantasy Island*, both about escaping normal life.

When I got older it was *Star Trek*. I liked the optimistic view of the future. I took Captain Kirk and Mr. Spock as my role-models.

On the baseball field and on the basketball court, I was Captain Kirk, emotional, yelling, hyping up my teammates. Off the court I was more like Mr. Spock, who never raised his voice. Spock was strong but in an intellectual way, cool and calm.

Hot and cold.

—

I had two separate friend groups. I excelled in basketball and baseball so most of my teammates were my friends. I was also a big nerd, into *Star Trek*, so I had my nerd friends. The nerds couldn't play sports and the athletes didn't want to talk about *Star Trek*. I wanted to do both.

In school I joined the Gamers Guild. Danny Che, Brayden Yu, Daniel Morris, and I would sit in Mr. Fair's classroom, eating potato chips and beef jerky, drinking grape Kool-Aid and playing Risk, Battleship, or Axis & Allies.

THROUGH THE FIRE

In junior high we started playing Dungeons & Dragons, taking turns as the Dungeon Master. On the weekends we would run marathon sessions and the hours, eight or ten of them, would click by as we got lost in the game, rolling eight-sided and twenty-sided die, working our way through the dungeon.

Our fellowship had dwarves and elves, wizards and warriors. It was a family where everyone was welcome.

We bought pewter figurines to serve as our avatars. I bought a knight with a longsword and painted a family shield on his coat of armor. In the world of Dungeons & Dragons I was a hero, protecting my family as we made our way through the maze to face the monster.

I knew there was always a monster waiting for you.

—

My bedroom was next to the master bedroom. I heard a commotion, and a then dull thump, a sound that made me think something was wrong.

I was seventeen years old, but I knew opening the door to their bedroom was a no-no. In my parents' house you didn't open closed doors. Their bedroom was empty, but grunts were coming from the bathroom.

There was always a monster…

My dad had my mom pinned against the wall by her throat, choking her. I grabbed him by his shoulder, spun him around, and punched him in the face as hard as I could.

My punch shocked my father and he let go of my mom. He looked at me, ugly and weird, and started laughing, a low, maniacal laugh.

We ran out of the room.

—

From Mesa Robles Elementary to Wilson High I was the best athlete in school.

I loved playing baseball, being at the ballpark, the big open space, the smells (the grass, the dirt, the taquitos cooking in the Snack Shack), the sounds (the cleats on the gravel, the ball into a mitt, the stomping of the feet, the crack of the bat, the chatter, "hey, batter batter,"), the dirt, sliding, hitting, fielding.

I was pitching so I had the ball in my hand a lot, and I was a power hitter, doubles, triples and home runs. There's a rush that comes with being able to put bat on ball and watch it fly over the outfield fence. The feeling of… solid contact.

There was so much downtime though, so much time with no action, between pitches, between batters, sitting in the dugout when it's not your turn at-bat.

Basketball was the opposite. You always had to do something. On defense, guard your man. Be ready for help-side defense. Rotate. Box out.

On offense, look for your shot. Set a pick. Pick and pop. Or pick and roll. Catch the ball and finish at the rim.

Basketball was fast-paced and fun. As I got older and learned the game, I started seeing patterns, how plays developed, how to get stops. I was taller than everybody, so I had that advantage and I had been playing for years against my older brother and his friends, climbing the fence and playing on the school's outdoor court.

Chip, my older brother, was a good basketball player, varsity for three years, but the more successful he was on the court the more abusive my father was to him off the court. All the shortcomings my father had he projected on to Chip.

I watched my father psychologically dismantle my brother, who retreated to alcohol and, eventually, drugs.

Watching this fueled my anger as I got better and better at basketball.

"Fuck you," I thought to my dad. "You can't take this from me. I am going to be good enough. I am going to play for the UCLA Bruins. I am going to play for the Los Angeles Lakers."

From sophomore year through senior year, I started for varsity. By the end of my senior year, I was 6'10", a high school all-American, and had led my team to the state championship.

—

One day my mom was driving me to a basketball game. We were on Colima Road, a two-lane road which led from Hacienda Heights over the hills to Whittier. Going up and over the hill felt like an escape, like leaving a dark forest behind us. The road was quiet, and I was relaxed, happy to be away from the house and spending time with my Mom. Playing on her eight-track was "Rocket Man" by Elton John. My Mom loved the song, had taught me the lyrics, and both of us sang together:

> And I think it's gonna be a long, long time
> 'Til touchdown brings me 'round again to find
> I'm not the man they think I am at home

For the first time I asked my mom, "Why don't you just leave him?"

"I'm going to," she said. "As soon as I get my kids through school."

That's when I realized my mom was worried about my Dad, worried about what he might do if she left.

I'm not the man they think I am...

She didn't say it at the time, but I think she already had a plan for how she would slip away.

Remember how the stars stole the night away...

Part II:
Chapel Hill

CHAPTER 3

Freshman Year

Dean Smith, small and confident, sat at our kitchen table.

"If you come to the University of North Carolina, I can promise you two things: one, you'll get a quality education and two, you'll leave a better person," he said.

An education and a better person. No other coach had said that.

After my junior year in high school, I played well at the Five-Star Camp in Western Pennsylvania and my recruiting letters changed from Cal State-Bakersfield to major programs like UCLA. Among the letters was a note from Dean Smith, Head Coach, University of North Carolina, the man who would change my life.

The man who would save my life.

Coach Smith was different from the other coaches who visited. Jim Valvano and his assistant coach, Tom Abatemarco, got into an argument in my living room when Abatemarco corrected Valvano. They were nose to nose. I knew I didn't want that. I'd had enough yelling in my life.

What stood out about Coach Smith, sitting at our kitchen table, was how down-to earth he was. He had won a national championship and an Olympic Gold Medal. He had coached numerous pro players, including my hero James Worthy and the current NBA sensation Michael Jordan. And yet Coach Smith wasn't over-selling the program.

He wasn't meek or soft-spoken but he also wasn't over-the-top. He was confident and humble at the same time.

A quality education and a better person. That's all Coach Smith promised.

—

My parents put me on a plane for North Carolina with $400 in my pocket, more money than I had ever seen in my life. My first day on-campus was a blur. I met Jeff Denny, my roommate, and his parents, Herm and Sue at Granville Towers, which was right on Franklin Street.

JD was a southern boy from Rural Hall, North Carolina. He wasn't a redneck, but he was country. Tomato sandwiches and sweet tea with so much sugar your teeth would shake country.

We hit it off right away. I used to tease JD about not being "city wise" until, over Christmas, we played in a tournament at Madison Square Garden. Walking around New York City I put some money on a game of three-card Monte, lost everything, and walked back to the hotel like someone had kicked my puppy. All morning I had been bragging about how I was street-smart.

"That dog don't hunt," said JD, shaking his head.

—

Granville was a series of three towers: East; West; South. All the freshmen and sophomore basketball players lived on the first floor of South Tower. Granville had an outdoor pool and an outdoor basketball court, and we played epic games of pickup, shirts versus skins, while girls sat by the pool watching us. I didn't know what I was going to major in but one thing I learned right away: when you're a Carolina basketball player you are a celebrity. For the first time in my life girls initiated conversations with me.

The students, the faculty, the staff, and the community knew basketball and knew all the players, even the freshmen, before we played our first game. We walked around campus wearing our light blue Converse sweatsuits, looking like big Smurfs.

At the center of Chapel Hill's campus are the old quads, green lawns and oak trees, surrounded by red brick buildings, rectangular and symmetrical. No cell phones or DM's back then so if you were in-between classes you headed to The Pit to hang out with teammates. We'd sit out there with all our Carolina basketball gear on trying to score a date.

Our seniors in '87 were Kenny Smith and Joe Wolf. Kenny was focused on being the best point guard in the country, focused on going to the NBA. Even though he was still an "amateur" according to the NCAA, Kenny set an example of how to approach the game in a professional way.

On the court Kenny was quick and clever, able to get to any spot and manipulate the defense.

"Set a solid screen," Kenny told me. "The better screen you set for me the better chance I have to gain an advantage. If your man has to help, you're going to be open on the pick and roll."

Joe Wolf wore a mullet and a smile. He was the first stretch four I ever played with, long before the term existed, shooting 58% from three that year. While Kenny was serious and focused Wolfie liked to party, drinking beer into the night on Franklin Street, usually at Four Corners or The Cave. There was a beer garden called He's Not Here that we all liked. I always thought that was great name for a bar: He's Not Here. They served beer in big, Carolina blue, plastic cups.

Purdy's, in the center of Franklin Street, was my favorite. You had to go down a narrow alleyway, and then up a flight of metal stairs. There was always a line, but we never had to wait.

After beers we would hit Timeout for chicken sandwiches. Because we didn't get bags of money like guys at some of the other programs, and because we had just spent the money we did have on beer, sometimes we couldn't afford the sandwiches but, for $1.50, you could buy a bucket of chicken bones and scrape off the little bits of meat.

—

During my freshman year Coach Smith gave a talk for students in Memorial Hall.

"I care about those I coach," he said. "Whatever you do, you need help. I'm not better than you and you're not better than me. We all stand equal before God. When someone comes up to me and asks for my autograph, I want to say, 'Can I have yours?

You got mine. I should get yours.'"

One student asked Coach Smith what he thought about basketball.

"It's just entertainment," said Coach Smith. "It's not going to change your life." [1]

We finished the year 32-4, 14-0 in the ACC. In the Elite Eight we lost to Syracuse by four points. Kenny and Joe were both drafted, Kenny going sixth to Sacramento and Wolfie thirteenth to Denver.

—

Each year, before our first day of practice we had to run a mile. Everyone had a certain time they needed to finish by to make the team. My time was five minutes and 45 seconds.

I had never run a mile in under six minutes.

"Holy shit," I thought. "I flew 3,000 miles to play for the University of North Carolina and if I don't run this mile in 5:45 I don't make the team."

One year Kevin Madden missed his time and had to train with the track team for the first week of practice.

I went around that track running scared. I could see the guards, Kenny and Jeff Lebo and Steve Bucknall, finishing, and I could faintly

---

[1] https://www.newspapers.com/image/67879304

hear the calling out of the times from the managers, but I didn't know how much time I had left.

I crossed at 5:21, amazed and exhausted.

My tough time, the time you had to make to get out of the first week of sprints after practice, was 5:15. In four years I never made my tough time.

—

Coach Smith ran everything in practice and his practice plan was detailed to the minute, from specific warm-ups to the small stations we would break into, to the shell drills to the guard and post work. The plan was taped up in the locker room. The most important parts of the plan were the Offensive Emphasis of the Day, the Defensive Emphasis of the Day, and the Thought of the Day. It was each player's responsibility to memorize all three.

At the start of each practice, Coach Smith would call on a player for the Offensive Emphasis of the Day, then a different player for the Defensive Emphasis of the Day and a third for the Thought of the Day.

"Okay, J.R., what is the Thought of the Day?"

If J.R. didn't know Coach Smith would say, "On the line."

One day we weren't crisp in practice. Coach had to leave early to do his weekly TV and radio show. He looked at assistant coach Bill Guthridge and said, "Coach Guthridge, run them until they drop."

We looked at each other like, "Oh my God."

"All right, everybody on the line," yelled Coach Guthridge.

We ran and ran and kept going, so dizzy and so tired and so sweaty and because you were so sweaty your skin would get cold even though you were sweating. Guys could barely run straight lines. Finally, Marty Hensley dropped and puked and I was like, "Thank you, Jesus".

Coach Smith made you a stronger person. You pushed yourself so hard you began to think that there was nothing you couldn't overcome in life.

All these years later I remember many of those Thoughts of the Day.

Never judge a man until you've walked two full moons in his moccasins.

"Scott," said JD, my roommate. "Coach is here to see you."

An eye for an eye and a tooth for a tooth leaves everybody blind and toothless.

I didn't understand. It was seven-thirty in the morning. Why would Coach Smith be at our door in Granville Towers?

In the end, it's not the years in your life that count. It's the life in your years.

CHAPTER 4

Tragedy

"Can you step out for a bit?" Coach Smith said to JD.

It was sophomore year, October 15th, 1987, the first day of practice. JD and I were getting dressed for our 9:00 AM class.

Fear rippled through me. *What had I done wrong?*

Coach Smith, wearing a Carolina warm-up suit, came into my mess of a room, sat on the edge of my bed and indicated that I should sit next to him.

"Well, he did it," said Coach Smith. "Your father killed your mother. They found him at the scene. He killed himself."

Coach Smith sat next to me on the edge of my bed with his arm around me as I held my head in my hands and cried.

Toward the end of my freshman year my mother had left my father. My dad was visiting me in Chapel Hill and, with my dad out of town and with the help of a friend, my mom and my brother packed up and moved out. Mom arranged to take some time off from work so things would cool down with Dad.

I knew my father was abusive but I didn't know he was capable of murder. *Why didn't I see this coming?*

Dad eventually tracked her down. He bought a gun, a .44 Magnum, and waited in the parking garage at her apartment complex. The gun held six shots. My dad shot my mom four times while she was still in her car and then turned the gun on himself.

I think he saved two shots for himself, in case he missed on the first one.

Coach Smith didn't say anything, just put his arm around me while I sat there with my head in my hands crying, both of us sitting on the edge of the bed in my messy dorm room. Even a man as brilliant as Coach Smith, what words can you say? Later, in his autobiography, Coach Smith wrote this was the most traumatic moment of his life.

The rest is a blur. Trauma punches holes in your mind, like an iceberg hitting the side of a ship. Memories drown in the sorrow.

I flew back to L.A. that day. Coach Guthridge and Mrs. Lee, the mother of the secretary for the basketball office, flew with me.

We had separate ceremonies for my mom and my dad and we buried them in separate cemeteries.

Mom was forty-years-old when she died. I'm older now than she ever was, older than my father ever was.

My brother and I had a falling out and I haven't had any contact with him for nearly two decades.

I'm the oldest Williams I know.

—

I asked Coach Smith about sitting out for the year.

"No," he said.

He never explained why, he just said, "No." I think he wanted me close and if I wasn't part of the team, he was worried I would drift away.

It worked. It worked for me to have a routine and structure and competition. Most of all to have the love and support of Coach Smith, my teammates, and the Carolina Family.

Healing is about connection and Coach Smith didn't want me to be disconnected from them.

My community, the Carolina Family, put their collective arms around me, held me close, and protected me.

CHAPTER 5

Carolina Family

Coach Smith's wife, Dr. Linnea Smith, met with me a few weeks after the funeral of my parents. She asked if she could arrange for me to see a therapist. I agreed but stopped after the second session. It wasn't productive for me at that time. I was getting more benefit from practicing with the team, preparing for the season, being with my teammates, and having to lock in on what Coach Smith was teaching. The two and a half hours of practice was better than 50 minutes with the therapist. And Coach Smith was right to not let me take the year off.

My teammates were a form of therapy even though they likely weren't aware of it. In the winter of '87 I had a lot of dark days. I never got to the point where I contemplated suicide but I remember many winter days in Granville Towers, when it was dark and cold out, closing the blinds and sitting alone, drinking, in the midst of deep depression.

When I was with my teammates and around my teammates, for those few hours of practice, my depression went away.

The extended Carolina Family swooped in to protect and comfort me. Angela Lee worked for the basketball office. Her mother, Mrs. Lee, would scoop me up and take me to dinner at their house. Her husband, Howard Lee, was the former Mayor of Chapel Hill. The Lees always seemed to time their invitations right. I'd start to get down and Mrs. Lee would call and say, "Come on over for dinner tonight. I'm cooking something up."

Sometimes after practice or games I'd sit in the outer office and hang with Angela. She had a prized plant that she kept green and healthy. One day I took a Sharpie and signed it. Soon everyone on the team had signed a leaf on her plant. It became a tradition for all Carolina Players.

From team to team, decade to decade, family and continuity has made Carolina basketball special. In his autobiography, Coach Smith wrote *Carolina Family* is "the thousands of small, unselfish acts, the sacrifices on the part of the players that result in team building."

—

Duke/Carolina is the biggest rivalry in men's college basketball. In the seventies and early eighties, Carolina kicked Duke's tail but by the late eighties Duke was on the national landscape of college basketball and knocking on the door to dethrone North Carolina for Atlantic Coast Conference supremacy.

In 1988 Duke beat us three times in a row and won the ACC championship, which was a shocker because we had owned them in '87 when we went 14-0 in the ACC.

It was embarrassing enough for a Carolina basketball player to show up in class the next day having lost to Duke. Now multiply that by three. Franklin Street was off limits. You went to class, and you went home. That's it. It's not like other students say "You guys suck" or anything like that. It's almost worse because people don't say anything at all.

You feel the coldness.

In 1989 Duke had the National Player of the Year, Danny Ferry, and freshman star Christian Laetner. During the regular season we beat Duke at Cameron Indoor Stadium and they beat us in Chapel Hill. Going into the tournament at a neutral site, in Atlanta, this game was our Alamo. We were making a stand to regain bragging rights, bragging rights that extended to the entire area.

The next day Washington Post reporter Dave Sell wrote, "There is no better rivalry in this conference than the one forged between the

Blue Devils and Tar Heels, and though they've played better fundamental games, few have been more intense."

The two communities, Durham and Chapel Hill, are only seven miles apart. Duke alumni and UNC alumni work together, see each other at their kids' soccer matches, are in line together at the grocery store. The entire geographical area, The Triangle, is invested in the outcome of a Carolina/Duke game.

Snell wrote, "North Carolina was ahead, 39-35, at halftime and was up, 43-39, when North Carolina's Scott Williams fouled forward Christian Laettner under the Duke basket. Smith removed Williams from the game, but as Williams ran by the Duke bench it appeared Duke Coach Mike Krzyzewski said something to him. Then it appeared that Smith and Krzyzewski exchanged a few words."

I was a physical player, setting the ACC record for most personal fouls in a career. I wanted the other team to know I was out there. If you're going to give me five fouls, I'm going to get my money's worth.

Fouls went both ways. If I gave a hard foul, I knew I was going to get one. We were all beating the hell out of each other. Under the basket I fouled Laettner hard, but nothing dirty.

Krzyzewski, the Duke coach, yelled at me as I walked by to the bench.

"Don't talk to any of my players," said Coach Smith to Krzyzewski.

"Fuck you," said Coach K.

Coach Smith was protecting me. It goes against the code for an opposing coach to yell at a player. Coach Smith never talked to an opposing team's players, regardless of what happened. He might talk to the coach, he might talk to the officials, but he wasn't going to yell at one of the other team's players.

It's classless.

Coach Smith stood up for me as would have stood up for any of his players. I fouled out in the second half, but we held on for the win as Ferry missed a three-point heave at the buzzer.

—

Each game, the last thing we said before we took the floor was, "Together." Before the game there were the X's and O's and game plans and schemes and scouting reports, but the last thing Coach Smith wanted us to remember is that whatever happened, we stay together. Guy makes a mistake, a turnover, air ball, the crowd gets on them, we don't splinter. If we fall behind, we support each other.

We stay together.

Carolina basketball is a family. If you were in Chapel Hill with me or before me or after me, there is a brotherhood and a bond much deeper than something like a college fraternity because we understand what it is to endure through all the training, all the sprints, the 220's and the 440's, the "tough time," running to the golf course and back, running the hill. If you endured all of that you passed the test and you belonged to the Carolina Family forever.

Coach Smith became the Head Coach at UNC in 1961. I played for him in the late eighties. When Coach Smith retired, he passed the torch to Coach Bill Guthridge, who was an assistant coach when I was there. From there the torch was passed to Roy Williams, with a brief intermission by Matt Doherty from 2000 to 2003. Coach Williams was an assistant coach at UNC when I was there and was the head coach from 2003 to 2021. From Coach Williams the mantle has now been passed to Hubert Davis, a former teammate I helped recruit to North Carolina. That's sixty years of a personal connection I've had to the program, from Coach Smith to Coach Guthridge to Coach Williams to Coach Davis.

—

When Hubert "Hube" Davis visited campus Pete Chilcult and I were assigned to show him around. Generally, the visits started on Friday, and we would get 48 hours with the recruit. The coaches wanted the recruit to spend time with the current players.

We wanted to immerse Hubert in the atmosphere: French Toast at Breadman's for breakfast, pizza and Ms. Pac-Man at Italian Pizzeria #3 for lunch, hang out on The Quad, steak dinner at Slugs, roll through Franklin Street, not trying to put on airs or ride around in fancy cars, just my little Honda Prelude, with all-black velour seats, or JD's Oldsmobile.

If a recruit asked a question, I gave an honest answer.

"Is it easy to play for for Dean Smith?"

"Playing for Coach Smith will be the hardest thing you've ever done in your life."

I'd tell them about the fifteen 220's or the timed mile or running to the golf course if we messed up or climbing stairs with a weighted vest.

"Don't come here if you think it's going to be easy, it's not. It's rewarding, it's fun, it's special, but it's not a cake walk. You have to be willing to put in the work."

Hubert may have been all skin and bones, a rail-thin freshman, but he earned our respect from the start with his competitiveness. It didn't matter if he was taking a beating and getting knocked to the floor, he always popped back up, ready for the next play. The team recognized this straight away. "Okay, you're not just Walter Davis' little nephew. You got some game."

—

We didn't have the best record my senior year, going 21 and 13, but I enjoyed being a senior. We had a number of freshmen who came in, Kevin Salvador, Matt Winston, George Lynch, who played a part in UNC's 1993 National Championship team.

Like Kenny Smith and Joe Wolf before me, I did my best to pass on the Carolina tradition. I enjoyed that role. Being part of a sports team is funny because, over and over, you go from being a mentor to being the lowest of the low. I learned from Joe Wolf and Kenny Smith and passed those lessons on and then, in Chicago, I learned from Paxson, Cartwright and Jordan and later passed on those lessons to players like LeBron James and Giannis Antetokounmpo.

There is a cycle to playing on a team where you start at the bottom, work your way to the top, and then, all of a sudden, the wheel spins around and you're at the bottom, trying to work your way back up the top again.

True in basketball and true in life.

—

Coach Smith had a large, rectangular office, papers stacked messy and high on his wooden desk.

After the death of my parents, I met with Coach Smith every couple of weeks.

We didn't talk about basketball, we talked about life. We talked school. We talked family.

One day I broke down crying, sharing with him my embarrassment that my father was a murderer. They say the apple doesn't fall from the tree. I worried people would think I had that kind of evil in me.

Coach Smith talked about his childhood in Kansas, and the pressure he felt to live up to his father's expectations, who had been a high school teacher and coach.

Although he was a busy man, Coach Smith always had time to talk. In many ways that was my therapy.

Sitting across from him, talking fathers and sons, tears rolling down my face, as Coach Smith shared personal stories and emotions from his childhood, I started to come through my trauma.

I think about Coach Smith every day.

This small, confident man, filled with decency, saved my life.

CHAPTER 6

Undrafted

Draft night, 1990, I was in my apartment with Jeff Denny, my girlfriend, and my brother.

After the first round I was both undrafted and embarrassed.

I went into my bedroom, closed the door, and watched the second round alone.

There was a total of fifty-four names called and not one of them was mine. I cried, heartbroken, watching my dream of playing in the NBA slip away.

I had a narrow window to make the league and it was rapidly closing.

—

JD told me about a summer pickup game Fred Whitfield had for his campers in Greensboro. Fred was a friend of Michael Jordan's and there would be several Charlotte Hornets' players and other NBA talent at the camp.

The game was for the campers and their family members coming to pick them up on the final day of camp. I signed on.

Charles Oakley was there. Muggsy Bogues. Bimbo Coles.

And Michael Jordan.

I met MJ the previous summer when he played pickup games at the Smith Center. He scored again and again on Steve Bucknell, our top defender. Buck was overmatched but who wasn't when they went up against the Black Cat.

Before the game, Jordan called everybody in the locker room and said, "We're here to play a competitive game of basketball. If you're not here to play basketball, please leave."

We looked around like, "Seriously?" but no one said a word. Jordan was the best player in the game. If he wanted to go hard, we'd go hard.

The game was competitive. On offense I set tough picks. On defense, I didn't give up easy lay-ups. I didn't dominate the game, but I held my own and wasn't getting pushed around.

Late in the game we were down by one point. Jordan shot and missed. I grabbed an offensive rebound but instead of going back up I fired a pass to MJ, who knocked down the game-winning jumper at the buzzer.

As Jordan and Fred Whitfield left the gym in Jordan's red Corvette, MJ called Jerry Krause, the Bulls' General Manager, and told Krause to give me a look. Krause called a few days later an offered me a spot on the Bulls' summer league team.

No guarantee of making the team. No guarantee of even being invited to training camp.

But…

I had earned an opportunity.

THROUGH THE FIRE

Part III: Chicago

CHAPTER 7

Training Camp

"We work hard here," said Jerry Krause, General Manager of the Chicago Bulls. "And if you're not prepared to work hard every day, you're not going to make it on this ball club."

Krause smacked his lips as he talked.

"I want winners," he said.

Krause was small and fat and acted as if he was the little king of everything, like he had a need to exert dominance over the tall, young athletic men around him. He needn't have worried. No one was going to outwork me.

"Hard work beats talent when talent fails to work hard," Coach Smith had said over and over again.

I had played well in summer league and was invited to the Bulls' training camp. There were seven of us vying for one open roster spot.

Seven of us for one spot.

The Bulls put the training camp invites up at a budget hotel just off the highway, close to The Multiplex in Deerfield where the team practiced. A van picked us up each morning and dropped us off each afternoon.

When we stepped on the court the vets barely acknowledged us. We were expendable.

Each night back at the hotel, resting my legs in a too-short bed, icepacks on my knees, I mentally reviewed what had happened in practice, what I had learned, and what I needed to do better next time.

Our head coach, Phil Jackson, had installed the Triangle Offense. The Triangle, created by our assistant coach Tex Winter, was a human chess board spread over the maplewood of a basketball court, each player reading and reacting to one another, each of us in constant motion.

The Triangle had well over fifty different positions so at night I visualized different parts of the Triangle, went over where my teammates would go, and what I was supposed to do. We had our own terminology: center opposite, blind pig, strong side fill.

I went over them again and again.

Center opposite. Blind pig. Strong side fill.

After a few days there were five of us in the van. A few days later it was just me and Ben Gillery, a power forward out of Georgetown.

Gillery and I beat the snot out of each other. He was strong, cutting my legs out from under me or elbowing me in the back when I went up for a rebound.

We went at each other with desperation, knowing this was our shot to make the league.

To succeed in the NBA you need three things: talent, professionalism, and smarts. He who adapted fastest won. From the neck down Gillery and I were similar: athletic, strong players from good programs. I knew my advantage would come from the neck up, from my preparation.

Gillery was often in the wrong spot, posting up when he was supposed to be screening down.

Center opposite.

Blind pig.

Strong side fill.

I flung these prayers up to the basketball gods.

And I set picks. And I dove for balls. And I ran my tail off. And then, one day, I was the only player left in the van.

I walked in the locker room and there was my red and white Bulls uniform, number forty-two, resting on a chair.

No announcement, no press conference, no conversation with Phil Jackson or Jerry Krause.

But I had made the league.

Now I needed to prove I belonged.

My goal was to keep working hard, to work harder than everyone else on the team. And I did.

I worked harder than everyone not named Michael Jordan.

The Early Years

Chip in checkered pants & cousins

Mom

THROUGH THE FIRE

Coach Young, Coach Hernandez & Mrs. Jackson

1986 State Champs

Mom w/ James Worthy

UNC Dorm Life

Upset The #1 Team On To The Sweet Sixteen

Ben, Lisa & Ava

Ava & Ben

Ava & Lisa

1992 Chicago Bulls

Jeff Denny & Michael Laufer
at Old Head Golf Links

Kate Longworth & Barry Buetel at Grand Canyon University

Final Four 2022 w/ Carolina Family

Giannis Antetokounmpo & Ben @MSG

Ben Guest

THROUGH THE FIRE

CHAPTER 8

Michael Jordan

"The goal is home court advantage throughout the playoffs," said Phil Jackson on the eve of training camp. "If we have home court, we can beat the Pistons."

For three straight years the Bulls had lost to the Pistons in the playoffs. The previous season, while I was finishing my senior year at UNC, the Bulls lost the Eastern Conference Finals across seven brutal games.

And Game 7 had been in Detroit.

Johnny Bach, an assistant coach and former Navy veteran, told me, "You hit everyone who comes across the lane." He wanted the team to be tough, to expect to be hit by the "Bad Boy" Detroit Pistons.

Home court was the mission and from the first day of camp Michael Jordan took no shortcuts. He was first in conditioning drills, first in sprints, first in one-on-one drills, two-on-two drills, three-man shooting competitions. It didn't matter. He was *always* first.

In addition to his competitiveness, Jordan was the quickest player I'd ever been around. He made micro-movements, sliding between cracks in the defense, and then using his athleticism to accelerate and explode to the basket, finishing high above the rim. On defense Jordan would embarrass anyone on the team, from point guard to center. In scrimmage, on the B Team, I would post up, turn over my shoulder for a jump hook and then, suddenly, somehow, the ball was bouncing against the wall of the gym. I never saw Michael coming in from help-side to block my shot.

A *hook* shot.

Occasionally, when he wasn't around, the other guys and I would call Jordan "Black Cat" because he was so quick, would appear out of nowhere on all areas of the court.

Coach Bach told me to hit everyone who came across the lane, to toughen people up, to acclimate the team to what the Pistons would dish out. Mama didn't raise no dummy but I also wasn't going to knock Michael Jordan down. It was one thing to be physical with Bill

Cartwright and Horace Grant, it was another to go at the franchise player.

"Putting a forearm into Michael Jordan is a great way to get released," I thought.

Early on in camp I let Jordan cut through the lane.

He stopped.

"Hey, that's your check," Jordan said, pointing at me.

"That's your check," he said again, aggressively, meaning I was supposed to check him with a forearm or shoulder, not give him a free pass through the lane.

Jordan was the best player in the league and he approached training camp like he was on ten-day contract, a superstar with the work ethic of the last guy on the bench.

"That's your check."

It was a brilliant show of leadership. Everyone else fell in line.

—

Some guys were afraid of Jordan.

He was going to come at you, and you had better be prepared to go back at him with everything you had.

If you didn't respond to the challenge Jordan would run you off the team. He wouldn't go to management and tell them to release you or trade you. No, he would just embarrass you in practice, over and over again, so much that you would either shut down or asked to be traded.

Dennis Hopson, our backup shooting guard, was a nice guy but he didn't want to compete with Michael. Hop liked the women, the cars, the fancy clothes. He liked the *lifestyle* of the NBA, but he had a cool cat mentality. He didn't want to dive for loose balls or get too physical.

Up against that attitude Jordan was a bull who saw red. In practice he would get in Hop's face, nose-to-nose, chin-to-chin, telling him, "You ain't shit, Dennis. You can't guard me, Dennis."

Hop would go through the motions, swiping at a dribble on defense or fading to the corner on offense.

"I'm going to bust your ass, Dennis," Jordan said. "You ain't gonna get nothing today, Dennis. You ain't gonna get nothing."

Jordan went out of his way to call him "Dennis," not "Hop" like the rest of us. Hopson hadn't earned Jordan's approval and Jordan was testing Hop, seeing how he would respond to stressful situations.

Hop wanted no part of that action and lasted one season with the Bulls.

—

The Bulls' plane had two card games. In the back of the plane Jordan and Pippen and the other high-rollers played Tonk for hundreds of dollars a hand. Up front the low-rollers, Stacey King, Will Perdue, B.J. Armstrong and I, played blackjack for a few dollars a hand.

Every now and again MJ would come up front and play with us.

"I'll be the bank," said Jordan. "Bet whatever makes you uncomfortable."

In the 2020 documentary *The Last Dance* Perdue said he felt Jordan came up front to play with us out of a competitive need to dominate everyone around him. He wanted to beat the guys in the back of the plane *and* come up and beat the guys in the front of the plane.

That's not how I took it.

Jordan was being a good teammate, spending time with everyone, talking basketball and league gossip, or the Chicago Bears game on Sunday, or, often, things that had nothing to do with sports. Fishing or travel or cars. The subject didn't matter. Jordan was making it a point to connect with his teammates off the court, hanging out with the vets in the back of the plane and the young guys in the front.

Like me, Jordan had learned under Dean Smith who taught us the leader can't be separate from the team.

Jordan knew it and lived it.

—

By the end of training camp my basketball shoes were worn down to the nub.

I called my agent to request some more shoes, but I was an undrafted rookie on a nonguaranteed, minimum contract. My agent didn't even bother to return my calls.

However, I had the biggest shoe salesman in the history of the game on my team and his locker was next to mine.

"Mike," I said. "I need some shoes, man. Do you think you could help me out?"

"Yeah, I got you," said Jordan. "No problem."

Two days later there were half a dozen pair of Nikes, plus gear, overflowing from my locker.

"Thanks MJ," I said.

I noticed everything was Nike's Air Flight line, not Jordan Brand.

"Why didn't you put some of your shoes in here?" I asked. "I can wear Jordans if you want. Help promote your brand."

With a smile, Jordan said, "Scott, as much as you want to be helping me, you'd only be hurting me."

—

One day after practice, between Thanksgiving and Christmas, MJ said, "Juanita's cooking dinner tonight. We're going to watch the game and shoot some pool. Be at the house at 6:30."

I was getting to know the other young guys, King, Armstrong, and Perdue, as well as some of the vets like Paxson and Cartwright. Perdue and I would go for lunch at a deli next to the training facility in Deerfield. King and I might meet up downtown at Excalibur or The Cotton Club. But, for the most part, I was alone. The vets had families of their own and they weren't thinking about hanging out with a rookie.

Jordan was the first teammate to invite me over for dinner, not out to dinner, but family dinner, a home-cooked meal. I think he invited me because he knew I didn't have anyone. It also wouldn't surprise me if Coach Smith had said something to Jordan.

I'd have good days but evenings were tough, lying in bed with no one to call. I was living the dream, playing in the NBA, on a good team with the best player in the league, but that didn't replace a phone call from your mom.

After the game guys would meet up with their parents or get a late dinner with their brother or sister. I was jealous of that.

And envious.

So, when the best player in the world, one of the biggest celebrities on the planet, invited me to his house for a home-cooked meal with his family it meant the world to me.

After dinner we shot pool. Tim Grover, Jordan's trainer, was with us.

"Scott, come train with me, man," said Tim. "I charge a hundred bucks an hour."

"I'm making minimum over here, dude," I said. "I'm going to stick with the free guy at the facility."

Tim has since worked with a number of NBA players, including Kobe Bryant and Dwayne Wade, and published several bestselling books. I imagine he now charges more than $100 an hour.

—

Jordan was a generous teammate.

I would be out with Armstrong and King getting dinner and, at the end of the meal, the waitress would tell us the bill had already been paid. Jordan had slipped in the back with a couple of friends, had dinner in a quiet spot, and paid our bill without us ever seeing him.

Or we'd be in the club and then, "Hey, Mike wants you to join him in the back. He's got a little roped-off section." VIP before VIP was a thing.

Jordan would be in the back with bottle service and we'd be like, "Dang MJ, this where the action is at."

—

When Mr. Jordan, Michael's father, came to town it seemed to ease Mike up a bit. The team loved having Mr. Jordan around.

Mr. Jordan was a huge Carolina guy, so he knew me.

"Scott, Scott, come over here," he'd say. "What'd you think about the game?" I knew he was talking about Carolina beating Michigan for the NCAA championship.

"We were too smart for them, Mr. Jordan," I said. "You knew Coach Smith was going to have the boys ready to play."

You could tell Mr. Jordan was proud of his son.

I was envious of that too.

Four months after the 1993 season ended Mr. Jordan was dead, murdered for his car and his watch.

I regret not reaching out to Michael when his father died. I was triggered, wrapped up in my own emotions, and didn't call even though we both went through the awful experience of having a parent murdered.

I believe grieving his father's death was the reason MJ retired.

The pain is hard. Growing up you think you'll have more time.

And then, one day, time's up.

—

In 2011 we had the twenty-year reunion of the first Bulls' first championship. By then I was married with two kids. I introduced my wife Lisa and my kids, Ben and Ava, to Michael Jordan, earning super-cool Dad points that night. They saw my name up in the rafters, on the championship banners in the United Center.

I saw Jordan again at Coach Smith's funeral in 2015 and then at Coach Guthridge's funeral a few months later. I asked for his number to help set-up a golf date at Pinehurst.

"Absolutely," Jordan said. "Done."

One thing about MJ is, if he can do it for you, he has no hesitation in making it happen.

He helped me get a date at Shadow Creek in Las Vegas and he helped me again at Pinehurst. That's not to say I wouldn't have had access but I wouldn't have been able to pick my spots, like Shadow Creek on a Friday afternoon.

If I called, I might get, "Tuesday morning, and we're going to tell you which Tuesday that's going to be." Now I could say, "This is when I want to play. Can you get me on Pinehurst, number two?" Normally, you have to make that reservation a year and a half in advance but one call to MJ and he calls the course and it's, "Yes, sir. How many players do you have?"

That's a whole different world right there.

—

When UNC made the Final Four in 2022, in Hubert Davis' first year as coach of Carolina, a couple of my teammates, and Ben and Ava, went to New Orleans to support the team. I hit MJ up for some gear and, as usual, he came through, sending UNC tracksuits, t-shirts, and shoes for everyone.

This time the shoes were Air Jordan's. The VI's.

Carolina blue, of course.

CHAPTER 9

Running with the Bulls

Scottie Pippen was a ball-buster. I think it's because he and Horace Grant had been manhandled by Charles Oakley when they were rookies. Pip and Grant never put hands on me, like Oakley did to them, but they would fire basketballs at me when I was trying to get the balls on the ball rack at the beginning of practice.

Despite my rookie hazing I liked Pippen and Grant. When you saw one the other wasn't far behind. They wanted to make you feel part of the group. Pip was always encouraging and a great defender. In his book *The Last Season*, Phil Jackson called Pippen, "The most intelligent defensive player I've ever coached." Pip could make life hell for opposing ball handlers, make them look like eighth-graders moved up to varsity late in the season.

Every now and then Pip would get beat and he expected Cartwright, Grant, and myself to cover for him. He had these big, hard, dry hands and, when I would rotate over and take a charge, he would rush over to pick me up.

"Way to go, Tank."

"Thanks Pip," I'd say as he helped me up with those rough hands. "Maybe use more lotion next time."

—

The first night of training camp, Phil, MJ, and Krause all talked about beating the Pistons. Not winning the championship.

Beating the Pistons.

In our first meeting of the regular season the Pistons cracked us by seventeen points. We would split the season series with them but by the time the playoffs began we were a confident team, the best version of ourselves, and they were running on fumes. We beat them in four straight games, a sweep, winning the first and fourth games by double-digits. We didn't let their bullying tactics get in our heads and, after the third game, they realized they weren't good enough anymore to compete with us.

With less than a minute left in Game 4 we were up by more than twenty points, on the Pistons' home court, The Palace at Auburn Hills. The doors to each locker room were at the other end of the stadium from the team bench. To reach *their* locker room, the Pistons had to walk by *our* bench.

The previous year, after losing in Game 7, Jordan and Pip and the rest of the guys shook hands with the Pistons. Shaking hands after a series, win or lose, was part of being a pro.

I was standing next to Jordan, with a towel on my shoulder, cheering the mop-up crew, when we saw four of the Pistons starters, Thomas, Rodman, Laimbeer, and Aguirre, walking down the sidelines towards us, shoulders hunched, defeated and walking past us quickly, like New Yorkers on a windy day.

They didn't even glance at us as they slunk off the court.

Jordan and I looked at each other in disbelief.

"It ain't nothing worse than a motherfucker who can't take an ass-whupping like a man," said MJ.

—

The Lakers were my hometown team, the team I rooted for growing up. Big Game James, Byron Scott, Magic Johnson. Now, as a rookie, I was on the court facing off against them in the 1991 NBA Finals.

We opened the series in Chicago Stadium where we had only lost six games all year. MJ missed a jumper that would have tied the game and we lost Game 1 by two, only scoring 91 points at home.

We won Game 2 by thirty-one points.

Also at home.

Afterwards, Magic said, "We came to do what we wanted to do. You lose by thirty or you lose by two, it's still just one loss. The series is 1-1 and we're going back to Los Angeles."

Winning by two points was the Lakers at their best. Winning by thirty-one was us at our best.

We got this.

—

In Game 5, we were up three games to one in the series, the Lakers focused on stopping Jordan by double-teaming him every time he caught the ball.

In the huddle at the start of the fourth quarter, Phil looked at Jordan and said, "If they're keying in on you, who's open?"

"Paxson," said Michael.

"Well," said Phil. "Find Pax."

When John Paxson was on-balance for a catch and shoot jumper, from seventeen to twenty feet, he was as fine a shooter as there has ever been in this game. Pax hit five straight shots down the stretch, all off passes from Jordan.

—

Champagne stings your eyes. The team celebrated in the locker room and then I found a quiet corner and cried.

So many highs and lows, like kisses and tears all at the same time.

Coach Smith called me and said, "I'm proud of you, Scott."

—

The summer after we beat the Lakers, I had shoulder surgery in L.A. at the Kerlan Jobe Rehabilitation Clinic. Byron Scott and Magic Johnson were also there doing rehab for various injuries.

One day I was lying on the padded training table with the physical therapist raising my arm and rotating my shoulder back and forth. I was working on getting range of motion back, a painful process that you have to do in small movements, when Magic walked up, took my wrist and said, "Let me do this session. I still owe him for stealing my championship."

"No, no," I said, with a nervous laugh. "Don't play like that, Buck."

"I'm just messing with you," said Magic, smiling.

A few months later I was in tears when Magic announced he had HIV. At the time, we thought it was a death sentence. Instead, he's still going strong, a testament to the power of science and Magic's positive attitude.

—

The Knicks borrowed the Pistons playbook and surprised us in the '92 playoffs, pitting their strength and physicality against our speed and athleticism.

I was a bundle of nerves before Game 7.

In the second quarter Xavier McDaniel tried to intimidate Pippen. Michael Jordan stepped in between Pip and X, getting in McDaniel's face, forehead to forehead. It was a powerful moment, Jordan standing up for his little brother on the court, sending a clear message: If you mess with one of us you mess with all of us.

I was on my second non-guaranteed contract but there was a clause that if the team made the Eastern Conference Finals, I would get a bonus of a hundred thousand dollars which was almost a third of my annual salary.

Even when we were up big at the end the game I was yelling, "Don't let up!"

—

In 1993 the Knicks took the first two games in the Eastern Conference Finals, beating us badly both games at Madison Square Garden.

After we lost the second game *The New York Times* reported Jordan had been gambling the night before in Atlantic City. That was the worst thing that could have happened to the Knicks because, for the next four basketball games, Jordan played some of the best basketball of his career.

Jordan is the game's ultimate winner. As long as you did your job, playing hard, running the floor, and setting good screens, he was going to take care of the rest.

The most memorable moment of the series was Charles Smith's four missed attempts at the basket at the end of Game 5. I have sympathy for Smith. He lived one of those nightmare scenarios the fan base never forgets. In Smith's defense he was trying to score on a combination of Michael Jordan, Scottie Pippen, and Horace Grant, three of the best defenders of all-time.

—

In '93 the Suns had the best record, they had home court advantage, they had the MVP in Charles Barkley, and they had two more All-Stars in Kevin Johnson and Dan Marjele.

We had the experience of playing in the Finals and knowing how to deal with the distractions that come with the world's attention. We knew how to separate that attention from the game.

Phil Jackson set a tone, telling us," We're going to go out there and win both games." And then he went out and said the same thing to the media.

Our mindset was, "Dude expects us to go win both games? Well, we got to go win both games."

In Game 1 we hit the Suns in the head with a bag of nickels. Their style of play was the opposite of the Knicks, open and free. It was easy for us to get good looks, both three pointers and at the basket. Even though we played in the East we weren't really an East Coast style team. We were at our best playing an open and free-flowing style.

The Suns had Barkley who caught his stride in Game 3 and stole the game in triple overtime. I played 46 minutes that night, the most I've ever played in one game.

—

In the final seconds of Game 6 Paxson hit an iconic three point shot to win the championship.

Everybody on the court touched the ball, from B.J. Armstong, the inbounder, to Jordan, to Pippen, to Grant, to Pax. It summed up everything we had done in Chicago for the past three years, all of us working together for one common goal.

I was happy for Pax because he had knee surgery early in the season and lost his starting job to Armstrong. Pax never complained, never whined, and was always professional. He had been solid all season long, helping us as a backup, supporting the starter who replaced him, and now, in the biggest moment, he hit the biggest shot of the game.

Paxson was the hero. It wasn't Jordan, it wasn't Pippen. It was one of us, the bench bunch. As the team jogged back to the bench, I grabbed Pax and lifted him off the ground.

" Dude, you did it!"

Three championships in a row. No team had done that in 27 years.

—

Phil Jackson and I were never close.

Paxson, Cartwright, and MJ, all had a different experience with PJ, a different relationship. One thing I learned early on in the league was player and coach is all it needs to be. It doesn't have to be what Coach Smith was to me at UNC. The NBA is a business so do what you need to do, play how you need to play to be successful, and that was it. Phil Jackson wasn't about to have me over to his house for dinner and he wasn't coming to mine.

I've played for a number of pro coaches, including several Hall of Famers: Larry Brown, George Karl, and Don Nelson. Phil was better than all of them. He was the best at working with the personnel he had, putting each player in a position where he could be successful by maximizing our individual strengths and minimizing our individual weaknesses.

—

A few days before the start of camp in '94 the team was called to the training facility.

Michael came in with Juanita and his agent, David Falk. Jerry Reinsdorf, the Bulls' managing partner, was there. MJ sat down at a table, microphones and cameras waiting to capture the moment, and announced his retirement.

"I just feel I don't have anything else to prove," he said.

Jordan was being pulled in so many different directions. Everyone wanted a piece of him. An autograph. A conversation. A photo. When I wanted to go to a White Sox game or a Cubs game or ride my bike on the lake front or sit on my patio and drink beers in the summer, it was easy. People might say, "Hey, what's up Tank?" and keep on moving. That's it. That's a nice level of fame. Jordan was so famous he was a prisoner, having to spend all of his time in hotel suites or eating with friends in the back of a restaurant.

Jordan wasn't burned out on the sport; he was burned out on fame and the emotions of having to carry his father's loss.

He needed what I needed, time to heal.

—

Toni Kukoc was Krause's guy.

It wasn't spoken about when Toni joined the team, but Scottie, Horace, Will, Stacey, B.J., and I were physical with Kukoc to see how he was going to respond. We had lost the game's greatest player and now Krause brings Kukoc in like he's supposed to be the next Magic Johnson.

I had even more of a chip on my shoulder after the '93 season because of my exit meeting with Krause and Jackson. Jackson said he didn't know what kind of player I was.

That hurt.

I'm the kind of player that helped you win three championships. You don't remember me playing 46 minutes in Game Three of The Finals a couple weeks ago? I'm the kind of player who went out there with a busted shoulder, his rookie year, and fought through subluxations and dislocations in practice and never missed a minute of action.

I was pissed off at Jackson and Krause because I realized then I'm going to have to leave Chicago, a place that I love, leave fans I love playing for, and leave teammates I love working with, because there was nothing more I could prove. I had played all twelve minutes of the fourth quarter of Game 6 of the '92 Finals. I had played 46 minutes of Game 3 in the '93 Finals. I had given my all, had been trusted in key situations, and I had delivered.

And yet Phil didn't see a role for me.

So that already had me pissed off. Then Krause brings in Toni. But shortly after Kukoc joined the team, we realized he was a good dude who was only here to work hard and to make himself and the team better.

—

The team traded Stacey King away to bring in Luc Longley. Luc was a big ole bucket headed, fun Australian dude.

Luc brought people together.

"Hey guys, I'm having a party at the house tonight. We're going to have some drinks and food," he would say. "Come on over."

—

In '94 the Bulls signed Steve Kerr.

Steve had been on the Cleveland teams we battled with in the playoffs. He was this short dude who had a good shot but couldn't guard a chair with rollers on it. I didn't learn until later that, like me, he had a parent, his father, who was murdered.

Steve was easy going, smart, quick to laugh. He fit my personality in that, when it's time to work you work but he also understood the game is supposed to be fun.

Basketball is a sport we *play*.

Steve and I had that same sort of attitude about sports and family and teammates. Maybe it's because of the shared situation he had when he was at Arizona and I was at UNC and we needed the support of our teammates to get through a difficult time.

Steve is going to be in the Hall of Fame as a coach. He knows how to deal with people, their quirks, different personalities. That was one of Phil Jackson's strong points and Steve shares that.

Years later, when I was interviewing with the Suns as a TV commentator, Steve, the Suns GM at the time, put in a good word for me and I got the job. Sometimes when the team was doing a film session Steve and I would get out on the court and play a game of HORSE. The rules were I couldn't dunk and he couldn't shoot threes.

I could never beat him, even if I shot hook shots and little turnaround moves in the paint.

—

No one gave us a chance in 1994 without Michael Jordan. The media didn't realize we were a team of competitors. With the addition of Pete Myers, a journeyman, and Toni Kukoc, a rookie, we lost two fewer games than the championship season team the year before.

The play everyone talks about from that season is the end of Game 3, against the Knicks, in the Eastern Conference Semi-Finals. Phil drew up the last shot for Kukoc and assigned Pippen to inbound the ball. Pippen refused to enter the game. Myers took his place and Kukoc hit the shot.

Afterward, in the locker room, Bill Cartwright was in tears over Pip's selfish act.

Years later, on T*he Dan Patrick Show*, Pippen said that he thought there was racism involved in Phil's decision to give the final shot to Kukoc.

Phil isn't racist.

Unlike other players, I didn't have a great relationship with PJ, and I have no contact with him today, but never did I think the man was racist.

He did carry himself with a superior attitude, like an arrogant professor when dealing with Pippen and Grant, whom he may have viewed as less educated. Sometimes he would poke fun at Pippen and Grant in a way that went over their heads. I wouldn't say anything, but I didn't laugh either, like some of the guys. Pippen and Grant were my brothers and I didn't appreciate Phil's teasing. I think that's one reason why PJ and I were never close.

But I don't think using Pip as the inbounder was out of any kind of racism. Pip was our best passer. Kukoc had made a similar shot in a similar situation earlier that year. PJ simply called the same play.

Later, in his autobiography *Unguarded*, Pippen retracted his statement about Phil being racist.

—

Jerry Reinsdorf was behind the breakup of the Bulls in 1998.

I was no longer on the team, but I had seen the dynamic for years. Reinsdorf, the owner of the Bulls, was the "good" cop and Jerry Krause, the general manager, was the "bad" cop. Behind closed doors, Reinsdorf made the decisions and then let Krause take the heat.

Reinsdorf knew he had the United Center sold out for two years. Krause was eager to show he could build a championship team from scratch.

They let Phil Jackson go, which triggered Jordan to retire, and then traded Scottie Pippen for a bag of chips.

Krause said, "Players don't win championships; organizations do."

Over the next three years the organization went 45 and 169.

The Bulls haven't made the Finals since they broke up the team.

By that time, I had left, signing a deal with the 76ers, who had Allen Iverson, a superstar with a terrible work ethic, the exact opposite of playing on the Bulls with Michael Jordan.

Part IV: The League

CHAPTER 10

Around the League

Sitting in the back of the Philadelphia 76ers team bus Allen Iverson, thin as my pinky, wearing a Reebok track suit, paged through *USA Today*.

"Clarence Weatherspoon makes more than me?" said Iverson. "How the hell does Clarence Weatherspoon deserves more than me?"

In the league talking salaries was a no-no but the paper had printed the salaries of every player on every team.

"Mark Davis, you only make $247,000? I didn't know you could get paid that low," said Iverson, laughing.

After the '94 season I signed a seven-year contract with the Sixers. Two years later the team drafted Iverson with the first pick of the 1996 NBA Draft.

"Scott Williams," said Iverson. "Scott Williams makes two point four million dollars?" "Enough," I said.

Iverson paused, smiled, and then kept reading our salaries aloud. He was the face of the franchise and could get away with whatever he wanted, even questioning the salaries of his own teammates.

Iverson was the worst teammate I ever played with. With all his talent Iverson only played fourteen years in the league. By contrast, I never averaged more than eight points a game, but I played in the league for fifteen years.

At practice Iverson would show up late and refuse to participate. All he wanted was to play in the games, score points, and get steals. Steals look good for an individual player but can be deceiving and, often, hurt the team. Iverson, defending at the wing, would gamble for a steal. If he got it, he had a breakaway layup but if he missed he put the rest of us in defensive rotation, playing four on five, and leaving us out to dry.

In team sports there is nothing worse than somebody who only cares about themselves, who doesn't care about team success.

On the Bulls, players showed up on time, knew the scouting reporting, and knew what the other players' tendencies were. Jordan knew the scouting report not just for the player he was defending but for everyone. In the locker room before the game Jordan would test our knowledge, quizzing us from memory.

Iverson showed up like he was playing rec ball. He didn't pay attention to the walkthrough, to what we practiced the day before, to how we were going to defend certain actions, or to the scouting report.

Iverson never got it. He wanted to win but he only wanted to win his way, where he got all the shots and all the glory. In his fourteen years in the league Iverson only made the playoffs eight times and, of those eight times, only got out of the first round four times. His image has been burnished by his team's one Finals run, in 2001, but the reality is Iverson was a selfish player whose teams often didn't win. And was disliked by his own teammates.

In Chicago we worked hard and were competitive, but we were also professional. There wasn't one fight between the players in the four years I was there.

In Philly, Iverson and Jerry Stackhouse got in a fight during *shootaround*.

After shoot-around, actually.

They were throwing up shots and then started playing one-on-one. The trash talk got personal and they squared up. Iverson threw a punch, Stackhouse hit Iverson and some of the guys broke it up.

I didn't move from the sidelines.

—

The Sixers practiced at St. Joe's off the Main Line. A few days before the start of training camp pros would trickle in to get a run.

One day, in 1995, there was a skinny kid on the court, working hard.

"Damn, this kid is good," I said to someone standing next to me. "Where does he play?"

"Lower Merion."

"What conference are they in?"

"It's a high school."

"Shit, I hope he's thinking about Carolina."

"I think he's thinking about the league."

Kobe Bryant, seventeen-years-old, was playing with some of the Sixers and some local Temple guys like Eddie Jones and Aaron McKie. Kobe wasn't the best player out there, but he wasn't the worst either.

A few nights later I saw Kobe and three of his high school teammates at Outback Steakhouse and picked up the check for them.

I always felt the league was a brotherhood. Pay it forward to the next generation.

CHAPTER 11

Always Be Pro

To stay in the league, you need three things: talent, professionalism, and smarts.

A lot of guys will have one or two and they can stay in the league for a little while but, without all three, they're not going to have a long career. Guys drafted to expansion teams, with no veteran leadership, might play four or five years on talent alone.

And then they were out of the league because they weren't taught what to do and what not to do.

—

When I came to the Bulls our vets were Bill Cartwright, John Paxson, and Michael Jordan.

Paxson was the point guard of the team. It was his job to get everyone to the correct position on the court. For the Triangle to work each player had to know more than one position. Cut off to the corner, accept the pass, pass away, shuffle cut, screen down, double screen for MJ coming off the weak side to the strong side.

Cartwright was the only veteran big on the Bulls. The other bigs, Will Perdue, Stacy King, Horace Grant, and I called Cartwright "Teach" because he taught us the tricks of the trade, little positions of the body, defensive angles, how to swing around an opponent to get in front of him, swim moves to beat a player boxing you out. Teach believed in using every part of your body to make life difficult for the opposing post player. Hands, forearms, elbows, hips, chest, and thighs were all part of the arsenal.

Stacey King was, like me, a young big on the Bulls. Whereas I was undrafted, King had been a lottery pick a year earlier. An All-American at Oklahoma and an All-Rookie Second Team in the NBA. Teach made up a flyer for the "Stacey King Skills Camp." It included finishing with your right-hand which King, a lefty, sometimes struggled with.

To the outsider this might seem mean, but Cartwright did it with the intention of motivating King, of helping him learn to be a complete player.

Cartwright, Paxson, and Jordan were the three leaders on the championship teams. They acted as an extension of the coaching staff but also an extension of the front office because of the way they handled themselves for media appearances, hospital visits, personal appearances, and any other team activities not related to basketball.

They set the tone.

"We're going to show up at this hospital at this time. We're going to gather here and then break off into separate rooms. We start on time, we end on time and you are going to not just be sitting there, you are going to be an active participant."

Cartwright, Paxson, and Jordan taught me "ABP."

Always Be Pro.

Always be pro in everything that you do around the game.

Be a professional because it isn't just about *being* in the NBA, it's about *staying* in the NBA.

One thing about being a pro is coaches want to see you make adjustments. For example, on a pick and roll, one coaching staff might want to see you roll inside and open up to the ball. Another staff might want you to immediately run to the rim. I can do it either way, it doesn't make a difference, but yesterday the coaches told me they want me to roll inside and then open up so I can see the ball. What they are really doing is seeing how quickly I can make that adjustment.

The coaches want to see if I'm listening, if I'm paying attention, if I'm coachable.

A lot of young guys will say, "Well, I scored, didn't I?"

That isn't the right approach.

Can you make the adjustment?

A professional can.

Always Be Pro.

That attitude propelled my fifteen-year career. My reputation as a good vet is the reason for my last few contracts and the back half of my career was about passing on the knowledge I had learned, helping players learn how to be a pro.

I never averaged more than eight points a game in my career, yet I played fifteen years because I was a *professional*.

—

Always Be a Pro also means that, sometimes, you have to have tough conversations with guys.

Michael Redd didn't have a lot of success early on in his career with the Milwaukee Bucks, a team I was traded to in 1998. Redd asked me what he needed to do. I took him aside for a private conversation, not in front of the team.

"You're a two-guard," I said. "You got to chase guys like Reggie Miller off screens and look at you, you're pudgy."

"Screw you," he said. "Why are you talking about my weight?"

"Your weight is working against you." I said.

The next year Redd came back in outstanding shape, made the All-Star game, and had a long career.

Nazr Mohammed was someone else who didn't always want to hear what I had to say. When he first came in, he didn't have post skills. He needed to work on his footwork, his agility, and his balance. Like Cartwright helped me, I helped Mohammad. He ended up playing seventeen years in the league.

Always Be A Pro.

—

I thought of my teammates as my family. Sometimes things get uncomfortable but we're a band of brothers and if there's an issue let's address it.

Part of veteran leadership is putting out sparks between players before they become fires. When the Phoenix Suns signed me in 2002 there had been several flare-ups between Penny Hardaway and Stephon Marbury. Each wanted to be the star of the team. They didn't understand the better the team did the better everyone does. Jordan was the star of the Bulls but because we won championships the spotlight was so big all of us were rock stars.

Hardaway and Marbury needed someone to put out the flare-ups and bring them together.

Putting out fires is about connecting with each guy and then getting them to connect with each other. What's the connection going to be with me and Marbury? He's a young guy from New York and I'm a vet from California.

Once, on a road trip in Los Angeles, my then wife Lisa and I wanted to have a date, so we left our young son Benjamin with Marbury and his wife.

Instant connection.

Where was the common energy going to come from with me and Hardaway?

We lived in the same neighborhood, so I suggested we drive to practices together. Now Penny and I were building a connection, especially since Penny is the slowest driver I've ever been on the road with.

Now how do I bring them together? Easy. By breaking bread.

I called them both and told them to meet me for dinner.

Steph showed up, Penny showed up, and now we were all at the dinner table and I'm buying so they can't walk away.

We started talking, laughing, and having a good time. We might have talked about how some family member always had their hands in your pocket, how someone's aunties car is always breaking down the first of the month.

Marbury and Hardaway were connecting off the court so now they start connecting on the court.

Before it was, "He didn't pass me the ball when I was open. I was supposed to come off for the shot. He did it on purpose."

Now it's, "He just missed me."

Before it was, "Oh, I see how it is. Next time I'm not going to pass him the ball." Now there was more forgiveness.

By building connection off the court, we created forgiveness on the court which deflates those little resentments, and extinguishes those little flare-ups, that happen on every team.

Connection equals communication.

In the huddle, instead of pouting, or ignoring each other, guys would say, "Let's talk about it. What happened in that last situation?"

"Well, I was coming down and I saw that somebody was being shaded that way and I felt I could beat them off to the drive."

"Okay, cool."

"Cool, I got you next play."

The team starts winning, fans are excited, more fans start showing up. It's a virtuous cycle.

A good vet puts out fires and plants seeds.

Trust is the fertilizer for these seeds to grow and the key to trust is communication.

Connection then communication then trust.

It's as simple as that.

I averaged 3 points for the Suns, and I started 34 games and we made the playoffs. Next year the team signed me to another contract because of the impact I had in the locker room.

Always Be A Pro.

—

Fifty-four players were drafted by NBA teams in 1990. Another few players, like me, signed as undrafted free agents. Let's call it seventy players total, from Derrick Coleman as the number one pick to the last undrafted guy who got a cup of coffee with a team on a ten-day contract.

Roughly seventy players made the league from the 1990 draft class. Except for one player, Hall of Famer Gary Payton, I played longer than anyone else.

After I retired, I called John Paxson and told him, "It was you and Bill and Michael who helped me be a better pro by following your example."

Those three guys helped me achieve my goals.

There has been a total of about 5,000 people who have played in the NBA. I played longer than 96% percent of them.

Not bad for an undrafted guy.

"Thank you," I said to Pax.

CHAPTER 12

Jordan versus LeBron

I'm the only player in NBA history to play with Michael Jordan on the Bulls and LeBron James on the Cleveland Cavaliers.

There are three other players who played with both Jordan and LeBron, but they all played with Jordan on the Wizards (Jerry Stackhouse, Larry Hughes and Brendan Hayward). I played with Jordan on the Bulls, when he was the league MVP, and I played with LeBron in his second year, when he finished sixth in MVP voting. I saw Jordan in his prime and LeBron on the verge of his prime.

It was the end of my career, the 2004-2005 season, my final season in the NBA, and playing with LeBron was a breath of fresh air.

He was so good.

He was also the strongest 19-year-old I've ever been around. In training camp in Cleveland, I took a charge from LeBron. As I hit the ground, I remember thinking, "I hope I didn't hurt this kid, he's the future of the franchise."

Bron popped up and ran down the court and my thought shifted to, "Hell, I hope he didn't hurt me."

—

One day, late in the season, LeBron and I were in the elevator going up to the practice floor. I could tell he was down. We would finish the year 41-41, tied with Washington for the eighth seed. The tie breaker went to the Wizards and we missed the playoffs.

"Hey kid," I said to LeBron. "It's gonna get better for you here. You've got the right stuff. They are gonna get some players around you and you're going to start winning." He looked at me and nodded.

—

On the team plane, an old 737, LeBron would sit across from me and ask questions while we played Tonk or poker.

"What was Phil like?"

"How did Jordan approach practice?"

"What kind of teammate was Pippen? How did he make sure everyone was involved?" Years earlier, when I was 22 and 23 years old, Jordan would come up to the front of the plane and play cards. Now, fourteen years later, on another team plane, LeBron was asking me about Jordan and how he led the Bulls.

LeBron was consumed with greatness, and with being great.

Years later, in 2016, LeBron would say in an interview, "My motivation is this ghost I'm chasing. The ghost played in Chicago."

—

Over the years I played with great players, Dirk Nowitzki, Steve Nash, Penny Hardaway, Ray Allen, Amare Stoudemire, and players the media considered great, like Iverson. LeBron was the first player who had the same work ethic, and the same drive, as Michael Jordan.

LeBron worked every day. No shortcuts. Just like Jordan.

"Hey, that's your check."

By the end of the season LeBron was a more vocal leader. He would pull a teammate aside, in the heat of the game, and correct mistakes.

"We're not on the same page with screen and roll coverage," he'd say. "Let's do it this way."

LeBron cared about his teammates, all of them. If LeBron signed a deal with Beats by Dre everyone on the team got Beats. If he signed a deal with Ray-Ban, everyone got Ray-Bans. LeBron was completely team-oriented.

—

They missed each other by a few months.

Jordan retired in May of 2003. LeBron was drafted in July.

Jordan has a summer camp he runs in Santa Barbara. After he was drafted, LeBron worked Jordan's camp.

"We used to play around 9 p.m.," said James. "The camp would end and we would stay along with the college kids that he would invite. We would get a good-ass run in for about an hour, an hour-fifteen. I was on the same team with MJ and we didn't lose a game."

They never played an official game though, never laced up a pair of sneakers and stepped onto an NBA court, facing each other.

Even if they did, Jordan would have been approaching 40 while LeBron was 18. Neither was in their prime.

The question, the debate, continues on in barbershops and internet forums, stoops and classrooms, pickup courts and podcasts: Who is the GOAT? *The Greatest of All-Time.*

Magic Johnson in 2020: When you want to say, 'Who's the greatest ever?' it's still Michael Jordan. Now, LeBron James' chapter is not closed yet. So maybe he has a chance to catch him.

Hakeem Olajuwon in 2020: When people start comparing (LeBron) with Jordan, then that's not a fair comparison. Jordan was a far more superior player.

Shannon Sharpe in 2020: LeBron is the only player in NBA Finals history to lead both teams in every statistical category. A guy that's pass first (LeBron) is the 3rd all-time leading scorer and a guy that's score first (Jordan) is the 5th all-time leading scorer. Let that sink in.

Charles Barkley in 2020: In my opinion, Michael is the GOAT.

J.J. Reddick in 2017: I think LeBron is the greatest player to ever play.

Oscar Robertson in 2010: LeBron's in a class by himself.

Rex Chapman in 2021: I think Michael's the best. Of course.

Skip Bayless in 2020: Michael Jordan is and will always be the GOAT over LeBron James.

Stephen A. Smith in 2018: LeBron James can never surpass Michael Jordan. When you lose six NBA Finals there's nothing to talk about.

Daryl Morey in 2020: People love to talk about this. For sure LeBron is the greatest human to play basketball. That's not even a question.

I played with both, with Jordan in his prime and with LeBron on the cusp of his prime.

When it comes to the GOAT debate, they are 1 and 1a.

But still, people want to know:

Who is the Greatest of All-Time:

Here's the answer or, at least, here's my answer.

They both have speed and stamina. They're both winners, they're both great teammates, and they're both professionals.

So, what's the difference?

LeBron wanted to *win*.

Jordan wanted to *beat* you.

LeBron didn't have that "I want to embarrass you" gear.

Jordan wanted everybody who watched the game to say, "That's the baddest dude I've ever seen put on a pair of sneakers."

And Jordan did it every single night. Whether it was on the biggest of stages, in Madison Square Garden in May during the Eastern Conference Finals, or in Sacramento in mid-November, on our sixth road game in ten nights because the Bulls were on our annual "circus trip" out west while Barnum and Bailey's took over Chicago Stadium for two weeks.

Jordan wanted the person in last row of the upper deck to leave saying, "Holy shit!

What did I just witness tonight?"

And he wanted that in every stadium, every night.

That's the greatness of Michael Jordan.

Michael Jordan is the GOAT.

THROUGH THE FIRE

Part V:
Through the Fire

CHAPTER 13

Little Victories

My mother wasn't a wallflower. She didn't back down from my father. She stayed with him to protect my brother and me.

When there is a murder-suicide in the news I always notice. More and more you read stories of a murder-suicide where the children are also killed. I don't know if that's why my mom waited until we were out of the house to leave, to protect us from our father.

—

I have difficult moments, especially around the anniversary of my mother's passing.

We all have our moments.

Life throws curve balls at you.

Your child gets cancer, or your partner gets hit by a car or your mother gets taken from you.

You can try to suppress it or run from it or drink it away but eventually you have to deal with your trauma, or your trauma is going to deal with you.

Once you make the decision to recognize and accept your trauma there's no clock for how long it takes to process and recover. Recovery takes time and patience, and you can't compare your recovery to someone else's. Everyone has their own trials to get through and their own journey to complete.

For me, I find little victories.

When I was having dark days in the months after my mother's death a little victory was going up to Franklin Street with a teammate and getting a burger and sitting down and being present and connecting with someone else.

Connection was the key. Connection to others. Just like in basketball.

The only way out of trauma is with the help and love of other people.

That's why Coach Smith wouldn't let me sit out.

Lately I find little victories in my kids, Ben and Ava. The last little victory I had was watching Ava, in her cap and gown, graduate high school. Ben chasing his dream of being in pro sports with the Austin Spurs.

Little victories.

That's how I keep going.

There's no great change.

There's no big victory.

It's just day after day of finding and celebrating little victories.

CHAPTER 14

$200

Dean Smith died in 2015.

We had remained in touch, of course. He came to my wedding and stayed long into the night.

A few weeks after his funeral I, and every other Carolina player, received a check from his estate for $200 with note saying Coach Smith wanted us to have a nice dinner on him.

It was the ultimate recognition that Coach Smith loved all of his players. He didn't care if you were Michael Jordan or Michael Norwood, he thought about you the same way, with the same love.

I never cashed the check.

It's in a frame on my living room wall.

I think about him every day.

CHAPTER 15

Ben and Ava

My son Ben and my daughter Ava are the source of my *greatest* happiness.

I feel bad that they haven't had love and support from my side of the family. There are no grandparents on my side, obviously. But also, no aunts, no uncles, I don't have any sisters, and my brother, Chip, hasn't been a part of my life since my son was nine months old. Chip has never met my daughter.

For years, I tried to help my brother, get him to a point where he could overcome the abuse he endured. But I'm not a professional and throwing money and love at him wasn't getting it done. After years of giving my brother a monthly stipend I told him, in 2004 during my last year in the NBA, when my contract ended, I would also end his monthly payments. That was the last time he spoke to me, nearly two decades ago.

Ben and Ava never met my mother, their grandmother.

I can see my mother in both of them. They have her spirit, her kindness.

As for my father, I want Ben and Ava to know that the cycle of abuse stopped with me.

I used to be embarrassed to have a father who had done such horrible things. It was one of the things I talked to Coach Smith about in our meetings. I worried people would look at me and think I could do those same things, that I possessed some of the same evil my father had inside of him.

Throughout my life I've worked with domestic violence centers, and I've learned about the cycle of abuse. My father was abused by his father, who was likely abused by his father. The cycle stopped with me and their mother and I have provided a different life for my children, filled with education and travel, support and love.

CHAPTER 16

Mom

There's a golf course I belong to in Ireland, Old Head Golf Links. When I walk the course, looking out over the water, I think about my mom.

If you could see me now…

I have conversations with her sometimes, in my head.

During the pandemic, traveling was difficult but in September of 2021 I finally flew out to California and sat at mother's grave and had a conversation.

I talked to her about life, my struggles, my hopes for my Ben and Ava.

It was good.

It was hard.

THROUGH THE FIRE

Sitting at my mother's grave I told her I went through a dark path, a terrible fire, but I didn't let it change the child she raised, the person she wanted me to be.

I played fifteen years in the NBA. I played with great teammates, including the greatest of all-time. I won three championships. I have two wonderful children, young adults now, who I'm so proud of.

You taught me to recognize when I made a mistake and needed to apologize, you taught me to care and to help others, you taught me to be the best person I can be.

You laid down your life for me and your strength protected me, even when you were gone.

You gave me what I needed.

I made it, Mom.

I made it through the fire.

ACKNOWLEDGEMENTS

Jeff "JD" Denny
The kind of friend you pray your children will have one day. Freshman year Coach Smith didn't just assign me a roommate he gave me a brother.

Celeste Milby
My aunt & second mom.

Herman, Sue & Richard Denny
Mrs. Denny promised my mother she would look after me while I was in school at North Carolina. Sue & "Big Herm" did just that for more than 30 years. They truly were my North Carolina family.

Butch & Kathy Miner

First Basketball Coach -HHBA

Coach "His" Hisatomi Mesa Robles Jr. High

Coach Lowe, Wilson High School

Coach Fogler, North Carolina

Coach John Thompson, Georgetown

Coach Bobby Crimmins, Georgia Tech

Coach Joey Myers, DePaul

Coach Rollie Massimino, Villanova

Coach Walt Hazzard, UCLA

A BIG thanks to all my UNC Coaches

Coach Phil Ford

Coach Bill Guthridge

Coach Dave Hanners

Coach Dick Harp

Coach Randy Wiel

Hall of Fame Coach Roy Williams, my first big man coach, who worked me endlessly to make my dream of playing in the NBA a dream come true.

Teachers & More

Mr. Long (Math)

Ms. Holiday (English)

Mr. & Mrs. Morris

Bill & Barbara Miller

Mr. Dwain Daniels Sr.

Mr. Young

Mr. & Mrs. Jackson

Ms. Angela Lee

Ms. Karen Lee

Mrs. Kay Thomas

Ms. Linda Woods

Mrs. Ruth Kirkendall

Catherine Frank

Burgess McSwain

Kendria Parsons Sweet

Mr. Bruce & Diane Weingarten

Mr. Barry Shipp

Wade Gaboriault

Thanks to all of my teammates from little league baseball & basketball, Wilson High School, North Carolina & NBA. I took many life lessons & found safe harbor on the fields, courts, carpools, locker rooms or homes.

Special thanks to:

Ben Guest
An excellent writer that's become a trusted friend. He knew when to push me to work & sensed when the pain was too much & backed off.